CONTENTS

GENERAL LEARNING OBJECTIVES OF THIS UNIT

This Open Learning Unit will supply you with all the core information you need to answer an examination question or to write an essay on the relationship between language and thought. It will take you three to four hours to read through, though it may well take you longer if you attempt all the suggested activities.

By the end of this Unit you should:

▷ understand the problems involved in explaining how we speak and understand language;

▷ be aware of the complexity of our thinking processes;

▷ understand the problems of separating out language and thought;

▷ know the main theories which have been proposed to explain the relationship between language and thinking;

▷ appreciate the practical implications of these theories;

▷ be aware of problems involved in researching the relationship between language and thought.

Introduction

Imagine travelling along a quiet country road on a clear, autumn evening. The sun is setting. The sky is many shades of pink, orange and purple. The trees are spectacular with leaves that vary from yellow and brown to reds, oranges and greens. A flight of grey and white geese passes overhead calling loudly.

Now imagine living in a society which only has words for black, white, red and green. How, then, could you describe this scene? Do you think that because you wouldn't know the names of the colours you wouldn't perceive them? Or would you be aware of them but not be able to describe what you saw?

This example suggests there is a relationship between the language we use and the ways in which we think about our world. It raises some interesting questions.

★ Do speakers of different languages see and think about the world differently? Or, to put it another way, does the language we speak affect the way we conceptualize our world?

★ Does language develop before thinking or can we think before we can speak?

★ Do language and thought develop separately at first and then come together later?

★ Can we think without language?

★ Does the language we use restrict or broaden our thinking?

Before we tackle these questions we must consider what we mean by *language** and *thinking**.

1

What is language?

KEY AIMS:

▷ To define what we mean by the term 'language'

▷ To explain how human language differs from animal communication

▷ An introduction to the types of knowledge we need to understand and use language

▷ To discuss current theories of language understanding

▷ To introduce a computer model of language understanding

▷ An appreciation of the relationship between schemas, language and thinking.

'It is a very inconvenient habit of kittens that, whatever you say to them, they always purr. If they would only purr for ''yes'' and mew for ''no'', or any rule of that sort, so that one could keep up a conversation! But how can you talk with a person if they always say the same thing?'

Lewis Carroll,
Alice Through the Looking Glass

Definitions of language

Alice's complaint about how difficult it is to communicate with kittens illustrates one feature of human language, the fact that we have the ability to use words in many different ways to express meaning. We use words as symbols which can denote both concrete objects, such as 'houses', and also more abstract ideas, such as 'justice'.

▶ Can you think of any other characteristics of human language?

Brown (1973) offers us a three-part definition of language.

Semanticity* He proposes that, to qualify as a language, a communication system must have semanticity, so that objects, events, emotional states and abstractions can be represented symbolically. That is, words must mean the same things to all speakers of a language.

Displacement* Second, communication about the past and future as well as the present must be possible. Brown calls this displacement.

Productivity* Third, it must be possible to combine a limited number of sounds or signs into an effectively unlimited number of messages. This is called productivity.

Do animals use language?

Clearly, according to Brown's definition, kittens lack productivity in their communication. But what about other animals? Many species communicate with each other through a system of symbols. For example, worker bees can tell other bees in their hive where to find a good source of nectar by performing a complex dance. Other bees interpret their movements and are then able to fly to the source of the nectar (von Frisch, 1950). However, unlike humans, the bee cannot communicate about the past and the future. It can talk about the present location of a nectar source from which it has just returned but this seems to be the limit of its abilities. Rabbits thump their feet to warn other rabbits of impending danger; birds develop systems of calls to tell other birds of the approach of a cat; dogs growl to signal 'beware'. But such signals do not incorporate the features of semanticity, displacement and productivity which are essential if a system of signals is to qualify as a language.

Human language

The system of signals used in human language is extremely complex. We combine individual sounds into larger sound units, words, which are themselves combined into even larger units, phrases and sentences, which are governed by grammatical rules.

Teaching language to chimpanzees Attempts to teach some form of human language to chimpanzees and gorillas have had some success. The animals learned to communicate at a basic level* with their trainers and even to invent some new vocabulary. For example, Gardner and Gardner taught Washoe, a chimpanzee, to use American sign language (ASL). Washoe quickly learned signs for individual words such as COME, TICKLE, GIMME and SWEET. She understood that the signs 'stood for' objects or actions so that when she saw a picture of a toothbrush or a person brushing their teeth she would rub a finger against her teeth. She also learnt the sign for MORE and used it in a variety of situations to indicate MORE SWEET or MORE TICKLE, although she did not always make the signs in this order. Washoe's most remarkable achievement was that she appeared to create new words by combining two signs together, such as WATER and BIRD to mean SWAN. Most of her combinations resembled those of her human companions, but she also combined signs in a novel way. For example, her companions referred to her refrigerator as the COLD BOX, but Washoe called it the OPEN FOOD DRINK.

This ability to combine signs to produce new words and phrases was demonstrated even more impressively by Nim Chimpsky (a pun, of course, on the name of the famous linguist Noam Chomsky), a male chimpanzee trained by Herbert Terrace. Of 20,000 recorded signs, about half were two-sign combinations such as MORE TICKLE, HUG NIM or MORE DRINK. However, once again, when the word order was examined closely, Terrace found that Nim was not consistent in the way he put signs together. Sometimes MORE was signed before TICKLE and sometimes after.

All the animals studied could cope with symbols and displayed semanticity, some displacement and a limited degree of productivity; hence, using Brown's definition, it might be claimed that they have acquired language. However, it is now thought that Brown's definition is too simple since it does not capture the complex grammatical structure which underlies human language. For instance, we all know that 'Throw me the ball' is a sensible sentence, whereas 'Ball me the throw' is not. By following grammatical rules such as this, we can talk about our world and, because they also know the rules, other people understand what we are saying.

3

FIGURE 1. *Nim signing 'dirty' in response to teacher's sign 'house' — meaning he has to use the toilet.*

We can produce innumerable new words and sentences which we have never heard or used before and, as we shall see, understanding and using language involves much more than simply knowing what individual words or combinations of words mean.

SAQ
1

(a) *According to Brown, which three features must be present for a communication system to be recognized as a language?*

(b) *Do systems of animal communication fulfil any of Brown's criteria for language?*

(c) *Which feature of human language is not displayed consistently by chimpanzees who sign?*

In this Unit we are particularly concerned with the cognitive processes involved in the use and understanding of *spoken* language. It is not about nonverbal forms of language such as gestures and facial expressions. Not does it deal with how we actually acquire our native tongue. This is the province of a separate Unit on language acquisition. What we are interested in in this Unit is the knowledge that we need to have stored in memory, and the ways in which we process that knowledge in order to be able to talk to and understand each other.

What kinds of knowledge do we need in order to use and understand language?

Linguistic knowledge

SOMETHING TO TRY

Read the following passage:

'Julie said goodbye to her friends outside the cinema and walked down the dark street. She heard quiet footsteps behind her. She turned her head and saw the tall figure of a man. Quickly, Julie crossed to the other side of the street. The man followed.'

Write a list of what you need to know to understand this paragraph.

Graphemic* knowledge First, we need to know that written letters of the alphabet stand for words and sentences with meaning.

Phonological* knowledge We need to understand how sounds are combined in English to form words. This is called phonological knowledge.

Morphological* knowledge Individual sounds, or phonemes, are combined into larger units called morphemes. For example, the word 'turned' has two morphemes, 'turn' and '-ed'. In English '-ed' is used as a marker to denote that the verb 'turn' is in the past tense. Similarly, the morpheme 's' added to the word 'friend' denotes a plural. So we need morphological knowledge.

Lexical* knowledge We also have to know what individual words mean. This is called lexical knowledge. For instance, to understand the passage, we have to know that a cinema is a place we can go to see a film.

Syntax* Another important factor is the grammatical structure or syntax of the words. As we noted earlier, chimpanzees seem to lack the ability to use words in the correct order whereas even very young children, apparently 'know' that you always say 'more orange juice' and not 'orange juice more'.

For instance, one syntactic rule in English is that sentences often start with the agent or subject, followed by a verb or 'doing' word, followed by the object or recipient of the action.

For example: She turned her head.
               Agent—verb—object

Semantics However, this type of lexical and syntactic knowledge does not give us all the information we need to understand the passage about Julie. In order to make sense of the paragraph we also need an understanding of semantics, or meanings, which are conveyed by combining sounds, words and sentences in a grammatically correct way.

The linguist's analysis of language

Why do linguists compartmentalize language in this way, rather than talking about sounds, words, grammar and meanings? Because they assume that we all have a grammar inside our heads which consists of the sound, word, and meaning patterns of our language. These patterns vary according to which language we speak. Linguists use the term 'grammar' to describe the knowledge we need in order to use and understand language and hypothesize about how phonological, syntactic and semantic knowledge is represented in the brain. They are particularly interested in our internalized syntax since they believe knowledge of meanings is derived from the way we combine the other components of our language. They use the terms 'phonological', 'syntax' and 'semantics' to differentiate between their description of our internalized grammar* and our everyday awareness of sounds, words and grammar.

SOMETHING TO TRY

Identify the phonemes, morphemes and syntactic rule in the following sentence: 'Jane likes apples'.

Social context Linguists concentrate on describing our internalized grammar, and we certainly need phonological, lexical, syntactic and semantic knowledge.

But we also draw on general knowledge about the world we live in. In the passage about Julie, we base our understanding of the story on the assumption that if a girl is walking alone in the dark, then a man following her poses a threat to her safety. Thus we place the story in a *social context** with which we are familiar. This suggests that our semantic knowledge must take into account more than the sum of the meanings of the words contained in the sentence. For instance, the sentence 'John gave Mary a ring' is ambiguous. It may mean that John had asked Mary to marry him or that he wanted to talk to her on the phone. Interpreting the meaning of the sentence depends on knowing more about the social context being talked about.

List the types of knowledge you would need to understand the following utterance:

'Look at the sky. Do you think we will be able to have our picnic?

General knowledge As we have seen, linguistic knowledge does not necessarily permit understanding of what is being said to us. We also need some general knowledge about the world which speaker and listener share. Sentences may be grammatically correct, but there are times when we don't have enough information to understand what they mean. To demonstrate what I mean, try the next activity.

SOMETHING TO TRY

Read the following passage:

'The procedure is actually quite simple. First you arrange things into different groups. Of course one pile may be sufficient depending on how much there is to do. If you have to go somewhere else due to lack of facilities that is the next step, otherwise you are pretty well set. It is important not to overdo things. That is, it is better to do a few things at once than too many. In the short run this may not seem important but complications can easily arise. A mistake can be expensive as well. At first the whole procedure will seem complicated. Soon, however, it will become just another facet of life. It is difficult to foresee any end to the necessity for this task in the immediate future, but then one can never tell. After the procedure is completed one arranges the materials into different groups again. Then they can be put into their appropriate places. Eventually they will be used once more and the whole cycle will then have to be repeated.

[Bransford and Johnson, 1972]

Now cover the passage and see how much you can remember about it. Did you find it difficult to make sense of what you read? You probably found it difficult to recall because you did not know what the passage was about. Now turn to page 47 to find out the passage's title and then reread the passage.

Bransford and Johnson (1972) used this passage to demonstrate that people are more likely to remember the gist of the passage when they are given a title than when they are not. Once you know what it is about you can use that knowledge to put the passage into a social context which gives it meaning.

A POSSIBLE PROJECT

You can try this experiment for yourself. Ask one group of people to read the passage without a title and ask them to recall as much as possible of what they have read. Repeat the experiment with different people but this time give them a title. Compare the recall of the two groups.

Pragmatics* Finally, we need to consider what we use language for. Language is normally used in a social context. When we talk to each other we are usually trying to achieve some aim. We might want to persuade our listener to do something, or to convey information or simply to show off. Whatever the aim, we use language to achieve our own ends. This is called pragmatics.

Speech acts*

Searle (1970) has studied these functions of language which he calls 'speech acts'*. Examples of speech acts are sentences such as 'Will you close the window?', a request; 'Be quiet', a command and 'It's a nice day', a statement.

SAQ
3

What sort of speech act is: (a) *Shut the door.*
                          (b) *Would you pass the salt?*
                          (c) *The dress is green.*
                          (d) *I apologize.*

Searle suggests that the way a listener interprets an utterance depends on what they think the speaker's intentions are. For example, 'Have a nice day' might be interpreted as sarcasm if it is said by your best friend as you leave for a particularly unpleasant interview. On the other hand, you would be more likely to interpret the same statement in its literal sense if you are just leaving for a day out with friends.

SAQ
4

Match the terms on the left with their meanings on the right.

lexical knowledge	*words or parts of words*
syntax	*rules governing meanings*
phonemes	*grammatical rules*
speech acts	*what words mean*
morphemes	*functions of language*
semantics	*sounds of a language*

Checklist

To communicate effectively we need:

1. Knowledge of how sounds combine to form morphemes [phonology]
2. Knowledge of how morphemes combine to form words [morphology];
3. Knowledge of word meanings [lexical knowledge];
4. Knowledge of grammar [syntax];
5. Knowledge of how word meanings are combined into meaningful sentences [semantics];
6. General knowledge about the world;
7. Knowledge of the context in which a conversation is taking place [social context];
8. Knowledge about the uses of language [pragmatics].

Theories of language understanding

Noam Chomsky's theory of transformational grammar*

The problem of how we understand what is said to us and how we are able to construct sentences which will be understood by other people is clearly very complex. The linguist Noam Chomsky (1957) argues that the human capacity for language is innate. The proposes that we must 'know' the grammar of our language so that we can work out the relationships between the words in any sentence we hear. By working out these relationships we can decide what the sentence means.

For example, we can recognize that the sentence 'Beautiful thoughts eat loudly' is grammatically correct even if it is nonsense, whereas the sentence 'Thoughts loudly beautiful eat' is nonsense and ungrammatical.

Chomsky has tried to describe the rules that allow us to produce all the sentences permitted in our language, but to date, neither he nor anyone else has managed to complete the task. Chomsky's theories have undergone enormous changes over the years as they have adapted to criticisms made by colleagues and to new findings.

However, a flavour of his ideas can be obtained from looking at the way he analyses the grammatical structure of a simple sentence such as: '*The girl ate the apple*'. This would be described using what are called rewrite rules. These are presented on the lefthand side of the page, with a commentary on what they mean on the righthand side.

1. S → NP & VP   The arrow means 'can be rewritten as'; thus this rule, when expanded, says, The sentence (S) can be rewritten as a noun phrase (NP) plus a verb phrase (VP). The NP is '*The girl*' and the VP is '*ate the apple*'.

2. NP → Art & N   The noun phrase can be rewritten as an article (in this case '*the*') and a noun ('*girl*').

3. VP → V & NP   The verb phrase can be rewritten as a verb (in this case '*ate*') and a noun phrase ('*the apple*').

4. NP → Art & N   This is the same rule as 2, but in this case the noun is '*apple*'.

Although these rules have been described with respect to a single sentence, in fact they have enormous generality. For example, a very large number of sentences have the NP + VP structure of rule 1, for example, '*John kicked the ball*', '*The very large woman sat on the whoopee cushion*', and so on. What this means is that a relatively small number of rules can generate a very large (in fact, infinite) number of sentences.

Things are, of course, more complex than this. In order to capture all the subtleties and complexities of language, Chomsky has suggested that language has to be analysed at a number of different levels (e.g. surface and deep structures). In addition, there are also different components to language:

— *Syntax*:   this is the grammatical structure which has been discussed in the preceding section;

— *Phonology*: this concerns the actual sounds of language, and the rules governing their use;

— *Semantics*: this concerns the meaning of a sentence.

Chomsky's theories provide an interesting description of the rules underlying grammar. However, these rules are to some extent idealized in the sense that they produce perfectly grammatical sentences. People, on the other hand, frequently do not.

SOMETHING TO TRY

Record a few sentences of yourself and someone else in normal conversation. Count the number of deviations from grammatical correctness, for example, unfinished sentences, sentences without a verb, and so on.

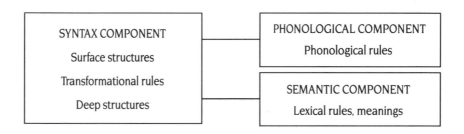

FIGURE 2. *Chomsky's model of language.*

Linguistic competence and performance A distinction is often made between competence and performance. Competence is what we are capable of achieving, that is, the perfect grammaticality of Chomsky's rules. Performance, on the other hand, is the language people produce, and is frequently less than grammatical, perhaps through lapses of attention or limited memory.

(a) *Analyse the following sentence using Chomsky's rewrite rules: 'The boy hit the ball'.*

(b) *What does Chomsky mean when he refers to the 'grammar' of our language?*

Do we remember the grammatical structure of a sentence or do we remember its meaning?

SOMETHING TO TRY

Read the following sentence:

'John liked the painting and bought it from the duchess.'

Johnson-Laird and Stevenson (1970) used this sentence to investigate whether people recall meanings of sentences rather than the exact words. When people are asked to recall the actual words used, their answers will tell us how they represent that sentence, either by the exact words or in terms of its meaning.

Without looking back at the original sentence, tick which sentence you read:

(a) The duchess sold the painting to John because he liked it.
(b) The painting pleased John and the duchess sold it to him.
(c) John bought the painting from the duchess because he liked it.
(d) John liked the painting and bought it from the duchess.
(e) The painting pleased John and so he bought it.

Did you find it difficult to remember which sentence you had read? Why?

Johnson-Laird and Stevenson found that many people tended to choose new sentences such as (b). This suggests that we tend to represent the meaning of a sentence in memory rather than its grammatical structure. Chomsky would argue that in order to extract that meaning, we have to analyse the syntactic relationships between the different parts of the sentence.

Computer simulations have tested the hypothesis that language understanding depends on meaning rather than on the grammatical structure of the sentences we hear but, before we discuss this, we need to consider how information about meaning is stored.

How do we store semantic information?

Schemas* Obviously memory is essential for storing information about people, events, places, things we are told, situations we experience and information we have read. In 1932, Bartlett suggested that human memory consists of schemas which can be thought of as packets of information representing our general knowledge about objects, situations, events or actions.

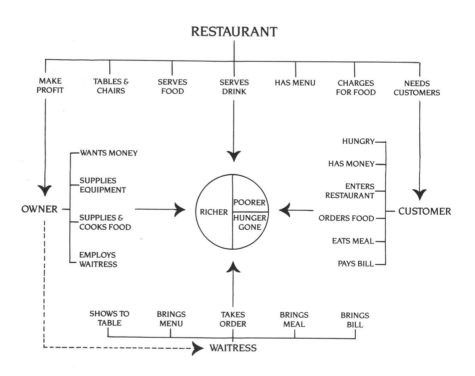

FIGURE 3. *Possible schema for a restaurant.*

Semantic networks* The question is, do we also store the lexical, syntactic and semantic knowledge which we need for speaking and understanding language in our schemas? Rumelhart and Norman (1983) suggest that we do, since all knowledge is stored in schemas in the form of semantic networks. These function rather like encyclopaedias in the sense that when we hear the word 'bird', we immediately think of other propositions* to do with birds (like 'they fly', 'have wings'), as well as names of different types of birds and personal experiences of them.

In this theory, language and meaning are inseparable in that the syntactical structure of language represents relationships between objects, events and situations which we try to match to information already stored in our schemas as the result of our past experiences with similar relationships.

Schema theory has been used as a possible explanation of how we use knowledge in order to interpret the meaning of the language we hear or read. For example, in Bransford and Johnson's experiment we can use our 'washing clothes' schema to help us make sense of the text.

Think again about the utterance 'Look at the sky. Do you think we will be able to have our picnic?' How does our picnic schema help us to understand what is being said?

Computer models of language understanding

Roger Schank and his colleagues have taken the idea of schemas and the way we use our general knowledge to help us understand language and tested the theory by means of a computer program. Schank suggests that many of our everyday routines are represented in memory in the form of 'scripts'*. By this he means that, as the result of past experiences, we build up a store of information about what is likely to happen in a familiar situation such as visiting a restaurant. For example, when we go to a restaurant we expect to read a menu, order food, have the food brought to us, eat the food, pay for it and then leave.

SOMETHING TO TRY

Think about what you expect to happen when you go to a restaurant. Imagine that you have to write a play about visiting a restaurant. Who is likely to be involved? What props would you need? Who gains or loses from the experience? Write the instructions for four short scenes under the headings ENTERING, ORDERING, EATING, EXITING. Use the restaurant schema to help you.

In Figure 4 you can compare your script with the one Schank wrote for a computer program called SAM (Script Applier Mechanism*). Note that Schank concentrates on how we draw on our schemas to understand language rather than on analysing sentences syntactically. He believes that syntax and meaning are analysed simultaneously. This is in contrast to Chomsky who considers that syntactic analysis must occur first.

Notice that SAM has two parts. In the first part, the computer is programmed with general knowledge about restaurants which includes the roles taken by different people, the props which are likely to be used, the reasons why someone might enter a restaurant and what the final outcome of the visit will be for each person involved. This is very similar to the information stored in our restaurant schema. The second part of the program describes routines which are followed when we go to a restaurant. We acquire this knowledge from past experiences of visits to restaurants.

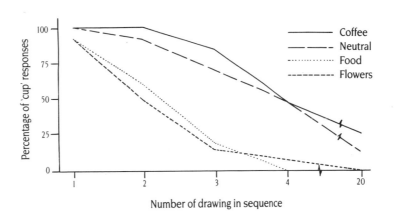

FIGURE 8. *Results of Labov's experiment.*

SAQ
9

What do the results of Labov's experiment tell you about each group's responses to naming the object?

Labov concluded that context influences how people conceptualize objects. Therefore, boundaries between some concepts must be fuzzy rather than clearly defined. Since Labov tested only concepts of everyday household objects, we cannot conclude that all concepts have fuzzy boundaries*. It is difficult to imagine the concept 'triangle' in mathematics having a fuzzy boundary, although if we count the diagrams in Figure 6a as triangles the boundary between triangles and non-triangles becomes less well-defined.

Rosch and Mervis (1975) suggest that we organize our concepts in terms of lists of features which are the most typical of that concept but that some of these features may also apply to other concepts.

For example, the carrot has been designated a fruit by the European Commission. To us, the carrot has many features which make it a member of the concept 'vegetable'. These include the fact it grows in the ground, is not sweet, you peel it, and it may be muddy when you buy it. But people also make carrot cake and the Portuguese make jam from it. Both features suggest that the boundary between 'carrot as a vegetable' and 'carrot as a fruit' is more fuzzy than we thought, since cakes and jam are more often made from fruit than from vegetables.

How are our concepts organized?

Rosch thinks our concepts are organized in hierarchies*, an example of which can be seen in Figure 9.

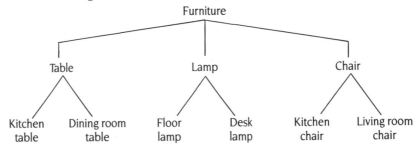

FIGURE 9. *Rosch's hierarchy for furniture.*

21

According to Rosch, when we use our concepts to think, there is one basic level which we select from the concept in order to communicate with other people. The level we choose depends on cultural factors. This means that we select the level which is best understood and shared by other people. With the concept 'furniture', the basic level we use is the individual items of furniture, because we know that people will understand what we are referring to if we say we wish to buy a chair. Our listener would be confused if we simply said we wished to buy a piece of furniture.

SOMETHING TO TRY

Draw a simple hierarchy for the concept 'vegetable'.

The role of expert knowledge

If we were speaking to an antique dealer, we might have to specify that we wish to purchase a Chippendale chair rather than any old kitchen chair. Rosch argues that knowledge is fundamental in how we conceptualize objects. The more expert we are, the more levels our hierarchies are likely to have, although being an expert does not necessarily lead to clearly-defined concepts. It does, however, increase the complexity of our conceptual hierarchies.

The role of language in concepts

At the beginning of this section I said we would consider the role of language in thinking but, so far, I have not mentioned it. The reason is quite simple. None of this discussion of the role of concepts in thinking would be possible without language. If we did not have verbal labels, we could not formulate concepts of abstract ideas such as justice or psychology. Without language, we would be unable to store complex hierarchies and would be limited to concepts based on images.

We need language in order to combine concepts for the purpose of complex thinking. For example, we can produce the sentence, '*Paul's passing his exams was a surprise to everyone*', which contains an extremely complicated set of propositions. First, '*Paul's passing his exams*' contains reference to the concept 'Paul', the concept 'exams', plus general knowledge about the what exams mean in our culture. The phrase acts as the proposition '*Paul passed his exams*', which acts as the subject for a second proposition within the sentence, '*It was a surprise to everyone*'. This complex embedding of one proposition in another would be impossible without language.

Acquisition of concepts

Bruner, Goodnow and Austin (1956) demonstrated that adults adopt various strategies in learning conceptual rules. Some focus on one feature of an object at a time and compare this with other, similar objects to see if they all have the feature in common. This is called the focusing strategy. Others form a hypothesis about all the features which comprise a concept, and compare this with other instances of the concept to check if their hypothesis is correct. If it is not, they abandon their hypothesis, form a new one and test it in the same way. Bruner called this a scanning strategy.

They argued that to learn the concept 'ball', children have to work out a conceptual rule to define what objects called 'balls' by adults have in common. Once they have worked out the features involved in the concept, children can then identify the class of objects which adults think of as balls.

This strategy of testing rules* is clearly illustrated when young children over-generalize. For example, they call all four-legged animals 'doggie' or all men 'daddy'. Adult responses either confirm or refute these rules, which children eventually modify in the light of their experience of different animals and men.

Critics argue that Bruner's experiment lacks ecological validity because the adult participants were required to learn new conceptual rules by working them out from an array of cards which was in front of them all the time. Children, however, do not have many 'ball-like' objects in front of them simultaneously so that they can work out rules for the concept 'ball'.

An alternative explanation

In Part 1 we discussed how schemas help us to make sense of language. Schemas develop from birth as we act upon our environment. They change and increase in complexity in the light of our experiences and enable us to adapt to our world. They supply us with information which guides our behaviour. For example, a baby may develop very early on a schema concerning the circumstances in which her mother will pick her up. This type of schema is present long before a child learns to speak.

Concepts must be part of our schemas as we grow up but schemas include other important knowledge about appropriate behaviour in certain situations which we have learned from previous experience of acting on our environment. Some schemas are based on physical skills such as sitting up or walking. As babies become toddlers these become automatic. Other information may be stored as images. For instance, at about 18 months, babies recognize the image of their own faces in a mirror (Lewis and Brooks-Gunn, 1979). As we grow older we store visual and spatial information about the world in mental models (Johnson-Laird, 1983).

Many concepts cannot be stored like this. They depend on our acquisition of language. For example, although you can form an image of the concept 'cup', you cannot do the same for the abstract concept 'psychology'. As adults, we have acquired an enormous number of concepts which form part of our schemas, many of which are represented in memory in words. The ability to use language symbolically to store information is fundamental to what McKellar called imaginative thinking.

(a) *Identify three ways in which information can be represented in memory.*

(b) *Why are concepts necessary for thinking?*

Checklist

1. Concepts help organize thinking.

2. Members of classical concepts share all their features; members of probabilistic concepts do not.

3. Concepts can be characterized in terms of family resemblances, rather than as prototypes.

4. Instances of concepts may be typical or atypical.

5. Some concepts may have fuzzy boundaries.

6. Concepts are probably arranged hierarchically, the complexity of which depends on our knowledge.

7. We select a basic level from our concepts in order to communicate with other people.

8. Language is essential for the construction of abstract concepts.

9. Combining concepts through language is necessary for complex thinking.

10. Children may acquire concepts by working out conceptual rules.

11. Alternatively, concepts may develop as part of our schemas.

12. Concepts can be represented in memory in a variety of ways.

Theories of the relationship between language and thinking

KEY AIMS:

▷ To investigate which develops first, language or thought, or whether they develop separately at first and come together later

▷ To find out if our schemas develop before we acquire language and, if so, what effect they have on our language

▷ To consider if schemas are synonymous with thinking and, if they are, whether the language we learn affects the way we think

▷ To appreciate three theories which attempt to explain the relationship between language and thought.

Three theories

Three possible views of the relationship between language and thought have been explored in attempts to explain the complex relationship between the two processes. These are:

Theory 1 Language depends on and reflects an individual's level of cognitive development.

Theory 2 Language and thinking develop separately until about 2 years of age, at which point they join and develop together.

Theory 3 Thinking depends on language.

We will consider each of these theories in more detail.

1. Language depends on and reflects an individual's level of cognitive development

Jean Piaget

In his theory of cognitive development, Jean Piaget argued that language is a consequence of the development of intelligence. Essentially, Piaget believed that the development of schemas is synonymous with the growth of intelligence which is necessary if humans are to adapt to their environment and survive.

FIGURE 10. *Developing schemas through active exploration.*

25

Babies and small children build up schemas from birth as a result of their active exploration of the environment in which they live. As they explore, they try to adapt existing schemas to cope with new experiences and, if this is not possible, they have to create new schemas to enable them to cope with the world. For example, babies have a 'sucking schema' through which they explore the world. At first they encounter the nipple which is pleasurable and they are encouraged to suck more. This schema is challenged when someone puts a finger in their mouth which does not taste so good. The schema is modified so that the baby discriminates between objects that are good to suck and those which are not. Later, the schema must be modified again when the baby has to learn to drink from a cup. When the baby is introduced to solid food, a new schema has to be created to cope with chewing. This will also be modified as the infant is introduced to new foods of differing textures.

Since development of intelligence begins at birth, well before a child speaks, Piaget argued that thinking and language must develop separately. A child learns to speak only when its cognitive development has reached a particular level, such as the realization that a stick can 'stand for' a boat, just as a word can 'stand for' an object. He reasoned that language is incidental to cognitive development and is simply a reflection of the child's level of intelligence.

Piaget argued that children's first intelligent thoughts cannot be expressed in language since they exist only as images and physical actions. He called this autistic thought.

Piaget claimed that early speech is egocentric*. This means that speech is used to express a child's thoughts rather than to communicate socially with another person. even when they are apparently addressed to an audience. For instance, a three year old building bricks into a tower might say, '*I'll put this brick on next. Ooh, it's wobbling*'. Even though the child's mother is present and responding to the child's speech, Piaget argued that the child's utterances are not directed towards the mother but are merely reflections of his own thoughts and intentions. Gradually, the child's speech becomes socialized to take another person's reactions and responses into account. When this is achieved, the egocentric speech of childhood disappears.

Criticism of Piaget Piaget did not take into account that language can help us adapt to our world. He underestimated how children use language to ask questions and learn about the world from other people. Think how restricted your learning would be if you could not ask questions or discuss things. What would we do without gossip and talking about why people behave as they do? This must influence our thinking about relationships and our culture.

(a) *According to Piaget, how does intelligence develop?*

(b) *Explain what Piaget means by egocentric speech.*

2. Language and thinking develop separately at first but then merge and develop together

L.S. Vygotsky

According to the Russian psychologist, Vygotsky, language and thought develop independently of each other at first. He too thought that children begin to think before they can speak. During the first two years, babies begin to think by developing schemas as the result of their physical actions on the environment.

At about two years, an important change occurs in children's thinking in that symbols are used to 'stand for' other things, for example, a piece of string 'is' a worm. Also speech begins to emerge. Vygotsky believed that, up to this point, thinking consists of actions, perceptions and images. He called this pre-linguistic thought*. Meanwhile, language development has proceeded separately in the form of practice and production of sounds necessary for speech in the form of babbling. This is pre-intellectual language* which has its roots in social interactions.

According to Vygotsky, there is a crucial point in development at which pre-linguistic thought and pre-intellectual language merge together and the child begins to think in words. To understand what Vygotsky meant, consider again what we mean by thinking. In Part 2 we said that one function of thinking was to help us solve problems. At the age of two, Vygotsky believed that children start to use the sort of verbal thinking which we use to solve problems.

When children first start to talk, Vygotsky argued that their language is egocentric in that they cannot distinguish between their thinking and talking for social purposes. They simply speak their thoughts aloud. Between the ages of two and seven, speech about actions and plans gradually becomes inner speech*, while spoken language becomes social*.

Vygotsky believed that egocentric speech does not disappear with the onset of speech for communicating with other people but that it continues in the child's head. He found that when six- or seven-year-old children attempted a difficult task, they would often resort to thinking aloud, 'Now what am I going to do?', which helps them to organize their thoughts.

Even as adults we sometimes resort to this. For example, when you have mislaid your door key you may say 'I remember having it when I came in from the shops. I went into the kitchen to put the shopping away so perhaps I left the key there'. As a result of this conversation with yourself you have organized your thinking and formulated a plan for action which tells you to look for your key in the kitchen.

Vygotsky's theory can be represented diagrammatically as in Figure 11.

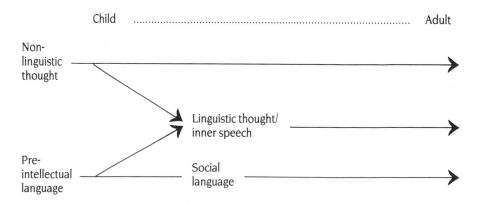

FIGURE 11. A *diagrammatic representation of Vygotsky's theory.*

How Piaget and Vygotsky differ

Piaget	Vygotsky
Language reflects individual cognitive development.	Language has its roots in social interactions, but thinking develops from an individual's actions on the environment.
Egocentric speech disappears and is replaced by social speech.	Egocentric speech continues in our heads as verbal thinking, whilst we develop social speech for communicating with others.

SOMETHING TO TRY

Observe a two year old and a six or seven year old playing. Listen to them talking and see if they use speech in the way Vygotsky suggests. Count the number of times they say aloud what they are going to do. For instance, do they say, 'I'm going to ride my bike', or 'I'm drawing Mummy'? Do they wait for an answer, or do they continue with what they are doing?

How many times do they say 'I' or 'me' at the beginning of an utterance? Is there a difference between the two year old and the older child in the way they talk?

The third view of the relationship between language and thought is the opposite of that adopted by Piaget and Vygotsky.

3. Thinking depends on language

The Sapir-Whorf hypothesis

Benjamin Lee Whorf, a fire insurance inspector, amateur linguist and student of Edward Sapir, a linguist and anthropologist, both reached the conclusion that the language we use affects the way we think. They maintained that the language we speak, through its vocabulary and grammar, determines the concepts we use in our thinking. Cultures vary in features of the environment which are important to their way of life. So each culture will have its own view of the world. For example, snow plays a fundamental part in the life of Eskimos and it is important for them to differentiate clearly among different types of snow. So Eskimo language includes words for drifting snow, fluffy snow, packed snow and so on. In fact there are 27 Eskimo words for snow.

Linguistic determinism Sapir and Whorf claimed that when children learn their native language they also learn a particular view of the world in the sense that a language contains words for concepts which are important in the lifestyle of that language speaker. Therefore our language must determine how we think. This is called linguistic determinism*.

Language determines thought or only influences it? However, not all proponents of this theory would support such a strong view. There are two versions of the hypothesis. The strong version states that language *determines* thought which implies that our language is totally responsible for defining our concepts. The second version is weaker and states that language only *influences* thought. This is called linguistic relativity*. The difference between the two is that the strong version suggests that if our language does not label, say, 'packed snow', then we will not be able to distinguish between it and 'fluffy snow'. The weaker version implies that we would recognize the difference but would not be able to talk about it.

SAQ
12

Go back to the beginning of the Unit and read the passage about the colours in a country road. How would you explain the effects of language on thinking in this passage according to (a) the strong version and (b) the weak version of the Sapir-Whorf Hypothesis?

Evidence for and against Sapir-Whorf

A classic experiment which supports the strong version was conducted by Carroll and Casagrande (1958). They studied the language of Navaho Indians which stresses the importance of the form of objects. For example, verbs used to describe the action of handling an object depend on the type of object being handled. Long flexible objects, such as string, have one word, while long, rigid objects, like sticks, have another. Flat, flexible objects like cloth have yet another word.

Psychologists already knew how American children developed object recognition. They first recognize an object by its size, for example a *big* ball. Once they have mastered this, they learn what colour the object is, a *red* ball. Finally, they come to recognize the form of objects, as in a *round* ball.

Carroll and Casagrande compared children who spoke Navaho with a group of American children who spoke English and a group who spoke both Navaho and English. All the children were the same age. They found that children who spoke only Navaho were better at recognizing the form of objects than either of the other two groups. They claimed this was evidence that the language we speak determines the way we think.

Surprisingly, they found the English-only group recognized the form of objects better than Navaho and English-speaking children. They accounted for this by the fact that the English-only children had benefited from nursery education. This finding has more significance than Carroll and Casagrande realized at the time. We shall return to it in Part 5.

SAQ
13

Why is Carroll and Casagrande's experiment evidence for the strong version of the Sapir-Whorf Hypothesis?

Other research on colour coding disputes Carroll and Casagrande's findings.

Colour coding

Not all languages have verbal labels for as many colours as we do. Some languages contain only two or four basic colour terms. This raises the question of whether speakers of such languages code colours in the same way we do, or whether their language restricts the way they categorize different hues.

Berlin and Kay (1969) investigated how different languages coded colours by presenting native speakers with an array of over 300 colour squares and asking them to indicate what words would be used in their language to describe each one. They were struck by the consistency between languages; all languages had at least two and at most eleven main colour terms (what Berlin and Kay called 'focal colours'*). What is more, the best example of each focal colour was the same regardless of which language the speaker used. For instance, the colour chosen as the best 'red' for an English speaker is also likely to be the best 'rouge' for a French speaker.

Heider (1972) investigated whether the colour terms used by different languages determine the ease with which colours can be discriminated and remembered. She studied the Dani of Indonesian New Guinea, who have only two main colour terms: 'Mili' which means dark and 'Mola' which means light. Despite the fact that the Dani did not have names for the focal colours such as red and green, they still found these colours easier to perceive and recognize than nonfocal colours. This is strong evidence that the language used did *not* influence colour perception.

▶ What can we conclude from this research?

▷ It seems that speakers of different languages find certain basic colours more meaningful than others. These are called focal colours. However, this does not mean that they are unable to perceive colours for which they do not have colour terms, only that they cannot give them a verbal label.

This is not to say that the language we use has no influence at all on the way we segment the world into categories depending on how important certain features of the environment are to our culture. It is possible that the effects of language are significant in areas other than colour perception.

(?) *How does research into colour coding contribute to the debate about the relationship between language and thought?*

Evidence for the influence of language on thought

Slobin (1979) draws our attention to the way some languages emphasize certain features of the environment which other languages do not. For example, French speakers distinguish between the familiar and polite forms of the second person pronoun 'tu' and 'vous', whereas in English we always use the neutral 'you'. The same distinction is found in German, where 'du' is the familiar form and 'Sie' is the polite form. Therefore, the French and Germans are obliged to constantly think about the social relationships between themselves and the people they are speaking to, whereas the English are not.

This does not mean that we are unable to consider the social relationship between ourselves and the person we are speaking to, only that our language does not emphasize the need to do so. In this way, Slobin proposes that our language must *influence* our thinking although it does not *determine* it.

Similar arguments have been expressed about the use of sexist language which will be discussed in Part 5.

(?) *Read the following passage in which Whorf describes how labelling drums as 'gasoline drums' or as 'empty gasoline drums' affects behaviour.*

... around a storage of what are called 'gasoline drums', behaviour will tend to a certain type, that is, great care will be exercised; while around a storage of what are called 'empty gasoline drums', it will tend to be different — careless — with little repression of smoking or of tossing cigarette stubs about. Yet the 'empty' drums are perhaps the more dangerous, since they contain explosive vapour.

[*Whorf, in Carroll, 1964*]

Explain how the language used to label the gasoline drums influenced people's thinking and behaviour in this passage.

Summary and conclusion

Evidence provided by Berlin and Kay and by Heider shows that the strong version of the Sapir-Whorf Hypothesis is probably overstated. However, the weak version — that language can influence but does not determine thought — is still a tenable idea.

5 Applications and implications of the theories

KEY AIMS:

▷ *To examine educational applications of Piaget's theory of cognitive development*

▷ *To discuss the implications for education of Bruner's emphasis on the role of language in thinking*

▷ *To consider whether some children enter education with a language deficit, or whether their language is simply different*

▷ *To investigate how sexism in language influences thinking.*

We have identified three views of the relationship between language and thought. We will now consider the practical implications of one view over another in two important areas — education and sexism in language.

Educational implications

Piaget's theory of cognitive development

Piaget's theory of cognitive development has greatly influenced teaching in primary schools.

FIGURE 12. *By manipulating real objects, children develop their thinking skills.*

Learning by doing Young children now mostly learn by doing. It is normal practice for children under the age of 11 to learn arithmetic with the help of concrete objects such as small wooden cubes and rods. For example, tens and units are learned with small unit blocks and longer rods which are equivalent to ten unit blocks. By manipulating real objects, the children develop their thinking skills. Piaget argued that children of this age are at the stage of concrete operations and that they can only learn to reason if they are free to manipulate real objects.

Pre-school and infant education operate on the basis that children's thinking advances as they encounter new experiences in their environment. To foster progress, discovery learning is encouraged in which children handle water, clay, and sand. By this method, conservation skills are gradually taught as children experience the properties of these substances for themselves.

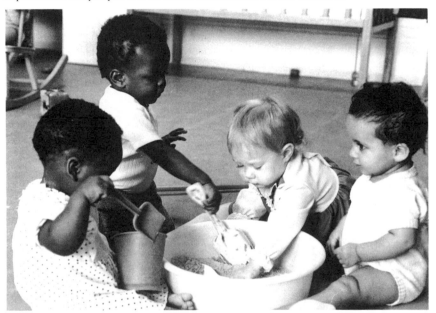

FIGURE 13. *Discovery learning.*

It is recognized that each child comes to school with a different set of experiences or schemas and the teacher has to build on each child's existing level of thinking. Since children develop at different rates, the implication is that the teacher has to assess each child's level of thinking and then offer appropriate experiences to promote further development. Notice that the emphasis is on doing rather than on language.

What role did Piaget believe language played in cognitive development?

Bruner's theory

Enactive representation* Jerome Bruner argues that language is essential for thinking. He believes that, at first, a child's thinking is based on its physical interactions with the world. At this stage, the child 'thinks' in terms of motor responses. It is as if our motor schemas are stored in our muscles. Examples include crawling, walking, putting objects into mouths, banging a rattle on a

33

tray to make a noise. Once established, these actions become automatic so that we do not have to think about them. Bruner calls this enactive representation.

Iconic representation The child then moves into the iconic* stage of development. Icon means 'image' in Greek. Bruner suggests that at this stage children begin to think in images. They can store knowledge in pictures, like photographs in the mind. He thinks iconic thinking begins at about the age of two. Now the child can 'imagine' its mother's face or what a cup looks like.

Symbolic representation* At six or seven, Bruner claims that children's thinking undergoes important cognitive changes as they begin to think symbolically. He argues that thinking with symbols depends on mastery of language. Without words, thinking would be restricted to what could be learned through actions and images. This implies that training children in the use of language will accelerate development of their thinking.

(a) *Which view of the relationship between language and thought does Bruner support?*

(b) *Why should improved linguistic skills help thinking?*

Is there any evidence to support Bruner's claim?

One study often cited in support of Bruner is that of Luria and Yudovich (1956). They investigated linguistic deprivation suffered by a pair of five-year-old identical twin boys in Russia.

The boys lived in an unstimulating home and rarely played with anyone except each other. They had received little encouragement to speak and their level of language development was primitive. In Bruner's terms, they had not developed to the stage of symbolic use of words. They did not use words to describe objects or events, or to plan their actions. They did not understand what other people said to them. The speech they did use was a private system of communication which only the two of them could understand. They did not appear to be mentally retarded but their play was very basic in that they never tried to build things or play imaginatively. Luria and Yudovich concluded that their language deficiency was preventing any more advanced or complex activity.

The twins were separated and sent to different nursery schools. One was given special language training, the other was not. Ten months later, the twin who had received language training had progressed more rapidly than his brother. However, both twins had learned to talk and their play had become more complex. Therefore, it is difficult to state categorically that special linguistic training had an effect, or whether both boys simply developed intellectually.

Perhaps the nursery schools gave the twins an opportunity to play with stimulating toys which, in turn, permitted development of more advanced schemas as the result of their experiences, or perhaps the fact they had both learned to talk was the influential factor. Note, however, that the twin who had received special language training made more rapid progress than his brother.

Look back to Carroll and Casagrande's study of the Navaho-speaking and English-speaking children. They found that the English-speaking children who had attended nursery school had more knowledge about the form of objects than the children who spoke both Navaho and English. Does this support Bruner's case? Explain your answer.

34

Is linguistic deprivation related to social disadvantage?

In 1961 the English sociologist Basil Bernstein developed a controversial theory in which he argued that different social classes use different linguistic codes or types of language. He suggested that the code a child learns at home may seriously affect educational performance.

Restricted and elaborated codes Bernstein claims that working-class children tend to use a restricted code*, whereas middle-class children tend to use an elaborated code*. Working-class parents are more likely to use words to direct and control their children rather than to explain why they should or should not do things. Sentences tend to be short, repetitive, limited in the use of descriptive words and are often grammatically incomplete. This is restricted code.

Stones (1971) illustrates restricted code by means of an imaginary conversation between a mother and child on a bus:

Mother: Hold on tight.
Child: Why?
Mother: Hold on tight.
Child: Why?
Mother: You'll fall.
Child: Why?
Mother: I told you to hold on tight, didn't I?

This conversation comprises short, repetitive sentences to control the child's behaviour. It offers only a limited explanation and assumes the child already knows what is being talked about. This is a feature of restricted code. It tends to be context-bound which means that it describes an immediate situation rather than exploring the past or future. For this reason, the speaker often assumes that the person being spoken to knows what is being referred to. For example, a boy might say to his friend 'He gave it to me' without explaining who 'he' is or what 'it' is. This information is often expressed through gestures and expressions rather than through words.

Restricted code does not express verbally the relationships between events and, according to Bernstein, does not allow the speaker to express abstract thoughts. In contrast, elaborated code places much more emphasis on descriptions and explanations of events. Sentences are grammatically complete and speakers tend less to assume that listeners will necessarily know what they are talking about. They use more explanation and describe past and future events clearly as well as the present:

Take another example of a conversation on the bus:

Mother: Hold on tight, darling.
Child: Why?
Mother: If you don't you'll be thrown forward and you'll fall.
Child: Why?
Mother: Because if the bus suddenly stops, you'll jerk forward onto the seat in front.
Child: Why?
Mother: Now, darling, hold on tightly and don't make such a fuss.

This is a more detailed explanation of why the child should hold on tight. Berstein believes that by using this fuller, more explicit code, the middle-class child learns to use words to articulate meanings in a way all listeners can understand. Elaborated code is said to express universalistic meanings*. This means that words are used to express events or ideas and the relationships between

35

them in such a way that everyone understands. The elaborated code speaker does not assume that a listener already shares his or her understanding of an event being described. Bernstein believes that language used in this way fosters higher levels of thinking.

Restricted code is said to express particularistic meanings*. In this case, the speaker is said to rely on the listener's existing knowledge of the situation to which the speaker is referring. If working-class children learn to speak restricted code, Bernstein thinks they will be disadvantaged at school since education demands the use of elaborated code.

Middle-class children go to school already knowing how to express universalistic meanings through the use of elaborated code, which is necessary for success at school. Bernstein maintains that working-class children are linguistically deprived since they cannot express themselves in the way the education system demands and so tend not to succeed at school.

A controversial theory

Bernstein's theory implies that the use of restricted code means working-class children are unable to think as logically as children using an elaborated code because of a language deficit which restricts their thinking. Use of the terms 'restricted' and 'elaborated' implies that elaborated code is in some way superior to restricted code. If you speak something close to 'Queen's English' you are thought to be able to think more logically.

SAQ 17

To which view of the relationship between language and thinking does Bernstein subscribe?

FIGURE 14. *Does the use of restricted code describe a language deficit?*

Does the use of restricted code describe a language deficit, or is it simply a difference in language use?

In 1970, Labov strongly challenged Bernstein's ideas. He studied black American culture which comprises a large number of socially disadvantaged families. He disputed Bernstein's notion that these families were in some way linguistically deprived and that this influenced their ability to think in an abstract way. On the contrary, he found that many children lived in verbally stimulating environments where they spoke Black English, a dialect.

Labov argued that speaking a dialect does not prevent abstract thinking. It is just that ideas are expressed in a different way. He also showed that the context in which language is spoken is important when considering whether or not people are capable of expressing abstract ideas. This is demonstrated clearly in his study of Leon, a young, black American boy who, when interviewed initially by a white interviewer, said very little. However, when interviewed by a black interviewer who spoke in Black English in an informal situation, Leon talked quite easily and proved to have many lively topics of conversation.

This emphasizes that the social situation in which a conversation is conducted must be taken into account when researching language use and understanding. Leon was quite at ease in an informal setting, talking to someone who communicated with him in the language he had learned to speak at home. He could not cope with the formal context of the interview with his first interviewer.

Labov criticizes Bernstein's theory of codes for not taking these factors into account. If a child is used to speaking what Bernstein calls restricted code in a very informal setting, then the same child will experience some difficulty in adjusting to the formal setting and elaborated code demanded by school. This does not mean that they cannot think about or express abstract ideas in any different circumstances.

Labov maintains that dialect speakers have problems at school because they have not learned the Standard English dialect of the education system in which success at school is measured. However, this does not mean that their thinking is necessarily restricted by their language, only that they do not know the language of formal education.

Williams (1972) devised the BITCH test (Black Intelligence Test of Cultural Homogeneity). This was designed to test the true ability of black children who spoke Black English. It was written in dialect instead of Standard English. When compared with white children matched for social class who completed the same test written in Standard English, they found that the black children performed as well as white children of the same age.

In terms of the implications for education, this suggests that some children come to school and have to operate bilingually in the sense that they have to learn the dialect required by the education system.

Conclusion

The theory of verbal deprivation is considered by Labov to be a dangerous myth in that it may lead to stereotyping children on the basis of their background or race. He does not deny that language influences thinking in the sense that children who speak in dialect have, in practice, to be bilingual if they are to succeed at school where Standard English is the accepted means of expression. Orr (1987) has found that children who use dialect are more restricted in mathematical thinking than Standard English users, which suggests that language does influence thinking. These theories have important and contrasting implications for education, particularly in multi-cultural schools, if dialect speakers are to succeed in a system based on speaking and understanding Standard English.

If you were a teacher, what difference would it make if you accepted Labov's theory rather than Bernstein's?

Sexism in language

SOMETHING TO TRY

Read the following passage:

A man and his son were apprehended in a robbery. The father was shot during the struggle and the son, in handcuffs, was rushed to the police station. As the police pulled the struggling boy into the station, the mayor, who had been called to the scene, looked up and said 'My God, it's my son!'.

What relation was the mayor to the boy?

Eakins and Eakins (1978) used the passage above to show how traditional forms of language can influence our thinking. Very few people who read this passage realized that the mayor must be the boy's mother. They also pointed out the extent to which women in our language are referred to as belonging to someone else, for example, 'Jim's wife', 'Ken's daughter'.

Marriage ceremonies declare that a couple are man and wife, again implying that a woman belongs to a man. People tend to think engineers are men and secretaries are women. Such examples draw attention to the fact that our language leads us to expect men and women to have different occupational roles, based on traditional, western stereotypes. Women are often portrayed as carers, while men are portrayed as 'owning' them.

This situation is reflected in our language. Men are described as being 'virile', 'strong' and 'assertive', while women are described as being 'caring', 'understanding' and 'attractive'. Such stereotypical thinking is mirrored by our language, which has few positive or neutral words for strong, assertive women, since these traits are traditionally thought of as masculine qualities.

FIGURE 15: *The Engineer.*

A similar situation pertains to sexual prowess. Men are described as 'virile' or 'potent' but there are no equivalent terms to describe a woman's sexuality. Also, there are over 200 English terms applying to sexually promiscuous women, but only 20 to describe sexually promiscuous men (Stanley, 1973). The inference is that we think sexual promiscuity is more 'acceptable' for men than for women. Thus our language can be said to reflect social thinking; but to what extent does it influence it?

Think back to the linguistic relativity hypothesis. You will remember that this suggested that the language we speak draws attention to certain features of the environment which are important to our way of life. This argument can be applied to sexist language which gives the impression that women are in some way inferior to men and are unimportant. For example, in English it has been customary to use the term 'man' when talking about people in general as in the statements, 'Man arrived on earth nearly three million years ago' and 'Man cannot live by bread alone'.

Schultz (1978) has shown that writers using this term were in fact frequently only thinking of men and that women were excluded from the term. Schultz cites a written example describing what people need in order to live. 'Man's basic needs are for food, shelter and access to females'. Spender (1982) argues that this use of language makes women 'invisible' and does not take into account their protective role as mothers in ensuring human survival.

Studies of the generic use of the word 'man' show that its use results in masculine images. When shown pictures of men and women described by sentences containing the generic 'man' or 'he', people agree that the sentences apply to all the pictures of men but many do not think the sentences apply to the pictures of women (Martyna, 1980). This demonstrates that use of the generic term is influencing their thinking.

Lakoff (1975) has shown that women are encouraged to use less assertive language than men. Boys rarely use tentative phrases such as 'perhaps' or 'I think'. They are taught to be direct and decisive in their language use, whereas girls tend to be less direct. Ervin-Tripp (1977) cites the following example of a little girl who has already learned that she is expected to 'beat around the bush' when speaking to a man but that she can be more direct when speaking to a woman. This reflects the traditional notion that women are not expected to be assertive in their relationships with men.

Girl to mother:	Mummy, I want milk.
Girl to father:	What's that?
Father:	Milk.
Girl:	My milk, Daddy.
Father:	Yes, it's your milk.
Girl:	Daddy, yours. Yours Daddy?
Father:	OK yours. OK it's mine.
Girl:	It's milk, Daddy.
Father:	Yes it is.
Girl:	You want milk, Daddy?
Father:	I have some, thank you.
Girl:	Milk in there, Daddy?
Father:	Yes.
Girl:	Daddy, I want some, please? [Ervin-Tripp, 1977]

Examples like this illustrate how children's thinking about gender-appropriate behaviour is influenced by the language they hear. They then behave in socially acceptable ways, one of which is to use different kinds of language, depending on whether they are a girl or a boy. The very fact that they do this will, in turn, affect their thinking.

The following extract gives further examples of language being used as a means of transmitting social attitudes to primary school children.

'Why, Maureen, you've had your hair cut, you look quite a young lady. Such a helpful child she always offers to put the toys away. A little boisterous for a girl but she's quieting down ... Emma, little girls don't fight like that ... Alex could you be very grown-up and take this over to the junior school to Mr Jones? ... he's a real little boy, you know, quite a tearaway at times.

[Primary teachers quoted in Eileen Byrne, 1978,
Women and Education, Tavistock]   39

As Sapir (1949) said:

All in all, it is not too much to say that one of the really important functions of language is to be constantly declaring to society the psychological place of all its members.

Research has demonstrated that the language we use influences our attitudes towards being male or female. This is why modern writers try to avoid using sexist language as, in English at least, women have been 'invisible' for too long.

SOMETHING TO TRY

If you have access to young children, listen to what they say while they play. Do boys talk more often about adventures and brave deeds than girls? What do the girls talk about? Does what you hear suggest that language influences these children's thinking and behaviour?

Checklist

1. Piaget's theory of cognitive development has led to increased stress on discovery learning in primary schools.

2. Bruner's emphasis on the role of language in thinking implies that developing language skills will facilitate learning.

3. Bernstein has suggested that some children may enter education with a restricted code which limits their thinking.

4. Labov maintains that the language of such children is simply different from that used by schools and that children can adapt.

5. Sexism in language influences thinking, particularly about our attitudes to being male and female.

6. Avoidance of sexist writing may help to prevent transmission of the idea that women are 'invisible' or 'less important' than men.

Conclusions

Clearly the relationship between language and thinking is complex. The processes we use to understand and speak our language involve more than 'knowing' grammar or vocabulary. We also need general knowledge about the world in which we live, knowledge of the context in which a conversation is taking place and about the functions of language.

In Part 1 we considered how this knowledge might be represented in memory as schemas. We then discussed Schank's computer model which demonstrates how we might draw on 'scripts' of events, developed from experiences of similar situations, to make inferences in language understanding.

Thinking is an equally complex process. In Part 2, we identified many different types of thinking which we use to help us adapt to our environment. We then concentrated on what McKellar calls imaginative thinking, which is the sort of thinking we need to solve everyday problems of living. Newell and Simon's General Problem Solver program, based on means-end analysis, demonstrates one strategy which might be adopted to solve such problems.

However, thinking involves more than ideas stored in words or simple cognitive maps. Johnson-Laird's proposal that we construct mental models of our world based on our experiences illustrates the complexity of our thought processes.

In order to think, we need to be able to categorize our world so that we simplify the massive amount of information which the brain receives through our senses. One way in which we do this is by organizing this information into concepts. Part 3 discussed how concepts comprise prototypes, typical and atypical exemplars, and how some concepts may have fuzzy boundaries. Research suggests that concepts are organised as hierarchies, the complexity of which are determined by the degree of expert knowledge we possess.

We also emphasized that many concepts would not be possible without language since they are based on abstract ideas. This led to the conclusion that much of the information stored in memory for use in thinking must be represented verbally rather than as images or mental models.

We discussed how children might learn concepts by working out conceptual rules, a possibility supported by their tendency to overgeneralize. Equally possible is the notion that early thinking develops through experience of acting on the environment. Concepts like 'cup' may be acquired as images, but more complex categorization of objects does not start until language is well-established.

The process of memory and perception are both used in thinking. We have to perceive objects, events and people in order to organize information about our world which we store in memory. We then use what we have learned about the world to help us solve new problems. We therefore have to be able to remember what we have learned in the past.

The relationship between language and thinking remains a matter for debate. Piaget thought that thinking or 'intelligent activity' preceded language. He believed initially that the emergence of speech simply reflected a child's level of cognitive development but later moved closer to Vygotsky's view that language and thought develop in parallel from different roots until the age of two years when they merge and develop together.

Sapir and Whorf proposed that language is fundamental to thinking since they believed that language either determines or influences thought. Having considered the evidence, we concluded that it is more likely that language influences the way we think.

In Part 5 we examined some implications of the views of the relationship between language and thought. Of particular interest is how primary education has changed in the light of Piaget's theory, and the extent to which language restricts or facilitates success in education.

Finally attention was drawn to the way that sexist language influences attitudes and thinking.

ASSIGNMENTS

Tutor Assessment

You are asked to write one of the following essays to be handed to your tutor for marking. You are advised to spend 45 minutes writing this essay, excluding reading and preparation time.

1. To what extent does language influence thinking?

2. Compare and contrast psychological theories of language.

3. Critically discuss two theories which attempt to explain the comprehension and production of language.

4. Use experimental evidence to consider the implications of the Sapir-Whorf hypothesis.

5. Discuss the educational implications of two theories which attempt to explain the relationship between language and thought.

If you have any difficulties with the essay, make sure you discuss them with your tutor.

FURTHER READING

AITCHISON, J. (1983) *The Articulate Mammal: An introduction to psycholinguistics*. London: Hutchinson. [Jean Aitchison describes attempts to teach language to animals and offers a detailed and highly readable account of Chomsky's theories.]

ATKINSON, R.L., ATKINSON, R.C., SMITH, E.E., BEM, D.J. and HILGARD, E.R. (1990) *Introduction to Psychology*, 10th edn. San Diego: Harcourt Brace Jovanovich. [Chapter 9 considers the relationship between language and thought by discussing concepts, reasoning and problem-solving in more detail than has been possible in this Unit. It also discusses how language develops and the difference between the production and comprehension of language.]

GREENE, J. (1986) *Language Understanding*: A *Cognitive Approach*. Milton Keynes: Open University Press. [The knowledge we need to understand and produce language is described clearly in the early part of the book. Judith Greene then discusses computer simulations of language comprehension, including Schank's SAM program. She also pays particular attention to the role of inferences in language understanding.]

GROSS, R. (1987) *Psychology*: *The science of mind and behaviour*. London: Edward Arnold. [Chapter 7 discusses the theories of the relationship between language and thought and considers experimental evidence which supports and refutes each theory.]

DOBSON, C.B., HARDY, M., HEYES, S., HUMPHREYS, A. and HUMPHREYS, P. (1981) *Understanding Psychology*. London: Weidenfeld & Nicolson. [Chapter 7 offers a broad outline of theories of the relationship between language and thinking, including a brief description of Bernstein's theory of restricted and elaborated codes.]

ROTH, I. and FRISBY, J.P. (1986) *Perception and Representation*: A *cognitive approach*. Milton Keynes: Open University Press. [This book gives further details of Rosch's work on concepts. It also describes Bruner's experiment on the acquisition of concepts and work by Collins and Quillian (1972) which draws attention to how semantic networks might be represented in memory.]

REFERENCES

Students studying psychology at pre-degree level, whether in schools, FE colleges or evening institutes, seldom have access to a well-stocked academic library; nor is it expected that they will have consulted all the original references. For most purposes, the books recommended in Further Reading will be adequate. This list is included for the use of those planning a full-scale project on this topic, and also for the sake of completeness.

BARTLETT, F.C. (1932) *Remembering: A study in experimental and social psychology.* New York & London: Cambridge University Press.

BERLIN, B. and KAY, P. (1969) *Basic Colour Terms: Their universality and evolution.* Berkeley, CA: *University of California Press.*

BERNSTEIN, B. (1974) *Class, Codes and Control: Theoretical studies towards a sociology of language, Vol. 1, 2nd edn.* London, Routledge & Kegan Paul. [Contains articles published between 1958 and 1971.]

BRANSFORD, J.D., BARCLAY, J.R. and FRANKS, J.J. (1972) Sentence memory: A constructive versus interpretive approach. *Cognitive Psychology,* 3, 193-209.

BRANSFORD, J.D. and JOHNSON, M.K. (1972) Contextual prerequisites for understanding: Some investigations of comprehension and recall. *Journal of Verbal Learning and Verbal Behaviour,* 11, 717-726.

BROWN, R. (1973) A *First Language: The early stages.* Cambridge, MA: Harvard University Press.

BRUNER, J.S. (1964) The course of cognitive growth. *American Psychologist,* 19, 1-15.

BRUNER, J.S., GOODNOW, J. and AUSTIN, G.A. (1956) A *Study of Thinking.* New York: Wiley.

CARROLL, J.B. (Ed.) (1964) *Language, Thought and Reality: Selected writings of Benjamin Lee Whorf.* Cambridge, MA: MIT Press.

CARROLL, J.B. and CASAGRANDE, J.B. (1958) The function of language classifications in behaviour. In E. Maccoby *et al.* (Eds) *Readings in Social Psychology,* 3rd edn. New York: Holt.

CHOMSKY, N. (1957) *Syntactic Structures.* Mouton.

CHOMSKY, N. (1965) *Aspects of the Theory of Syntax.* MIT Press.

ERVIN-TRIPP, S. and MITCHELL-KERNAN, C. (Eds) (1977) *Child Discourse.* London: Academic Press.

GARDNER, A.R. and GARDNER, B. (1969) Teaching sign language to a chimpanzee. *Science,* 165, 664-667.

HEIDER, E.R. (1972) Universals in colour meaning and memory. *Experimental Psychology,* 93, 10-20.

JOHNSON-LAIRD, P.N. (1983) *Mental models.* Cambridge, MA: Harvard University Press.

JOHNSON-LAIRD, P.N. and STEVENSON, R. (1970) Memory for syntax. *Nature,* 227, 412.

LABOV, W. (1970) The logic of non-standard English. In F. Williams (Ed.) *Language and Poverty: Perspectives on a theme.* Chicago, Markham Publishing Co.

LABOV, W. (1973) The boundaries of words and their meanings. In C.J.N Bailey and R.W. Shuy (Eds.), *New Ways of Analysing Variations in English.* Washington, DC: Georgetown University Press.

LAKOFF, R. (1975) *Language and Women's Place.* New York, Harper & Row.

LEWIS, M. and BROOKS-GUNN, J. (1979) *Social Cognition and the Acquisition of Self.* London: Plenum Press.

LURIA, A.R. and YUDOVICH, F.I. (1971) *Speech and the Development of Mental Processes in the Child.* Harmondsworth: Penguin.

MARTYNA, W. (1982) *The woman question,* In P. Mayes (1986) *Sociology in Focus: Gender.* New York: Longman.

McKELLAR, P. (1957) *Imagination and Thinking: A psychological analysis.* Cohen & West.

NEWELL, A., SHAW, J.C. and SIMON, H.A. (1958) Elements of a theory of human problem solving, *Psychological Review*, 65, 151-166.

PIAGET, J. (1950) *The Psychology of Intelligence*. London: Routledge & Kegan Paul.

PIAGET, J. (1959) *The Language and Thought of the Child*. London: Routledge & Kegan Paul.

ROSCH, E. (1973) On the internal structures of perceptual and semantic categories. In T.E. Moore (Ed.) *Cognitive Development and the Acquisition of Language*. Academic Press.

ROSCH, E. (1975) Cognitive representations of semantic categories. *Journal of Experimental Psychology*, 104, No. 3, 192-233.

ROSCH, E. and MERVIS, C.B. (1975) Family resemblance studies in the internal structure of categories. *Cognitive Psychology*, 7, 573-605.

RUMELHART, D.E. and NORMAN, D.A. (1983) Representation of Knowledge. In A.M. Aitkenhead and J.M. Slack (Eds.) (1985) *Issues in Cognitive Modelling*. London: Lawrence Erlbaum Associates.

SAPIR, E. (1949) *Language, Culture and Personality: Selected essays*. Berkeley, University of California Press.

SCHANK, R.C. and ABELSON, R.P. (1977) *Scripts, plans and knowledge*. In P.N. Johnson-Laird and P.C. Wason (Eds.) (1977) *Thinking: Readings in cognitive science*. Cambridge: Cambridge University Press.

SEARLE, J. (1970) *Speech Acts*. Cambridge: Cambridge University Press.

SLOBIN, D.I. (1979) *Psycholinguistics*, 2nd edn. Glenview, Ill: Foresman & Co.

SPENDER, D. (1982) *Invisible Women: The schooling scandal*. Writers & Readers Publishing Co-operative.

STONES, E. (1971) *Educational Psychology*. London: Methuen.

TERRACE, H.S. (1979) How Nim Chimpsky changed my mind. *Psychology Today, November 1979*, 65-76.

TOLMAN, E.C. (1948) Principles of purposive behaviour. In S. Koch (Ed.) *Psychology: A study of a science*. McGraw-Hill.

VON FRISCH, K. (1950) *Bees: Their vision, chemical sense and language*. Ithaca: Cornell University Press.

VYGOTSKY, L.S. (1962) *Thought and Language*. MIT Press.

WHORF, B.L. see CARROLL, J.B. (1964).

WILLIAMS (1972) Black Intelligence Test of Cultural Homogeneity. Referred to in R. Gross (1987) *Psychology: The science of mind and behaviour*. London: Edward Arnold.

GLOSSARY [Terms in bold type also appear as a separate entry]

Autistic thinking: term used by McKellar to describe the type of thinking used when we daydream. It was also used by Piaget to describe children's pre-verbal thinking.

Basic level: the level of a concept selected in order to communicate with other people.

Classical concept: a concept in which all members share the same features.

Conceptual hierarchy: the way in which concepts are organized, with superordinate concepts at the top and subordinate concepts at the bottom. The number of levels will depend on an individual's knowledge.

Conceptual rules: rules pertaining to features of objects which allow their classification as members of a concept.

Creative thinking: the type of thinking used by artists and scientists to create new ideas and works of art.

Displacement: the ability to talk about the past and future as well as the present.

Egocentric speech: Piaget's term describing children's early speech which is used to express their own thoughts and intentions, rather than for communicating with other people.

Elaborated code: Bernstein's term for the type of linguistic code said to be used by middle-class children. It is said to express universalistic meanings.

Enactive representation: in Bruner's terms, children's early thinking is based on their physical interactions with the environment.

Family resemblance: like members of a family, members of a concept share features with each other but there may be no feature which is common to all members.

Focal colours: colours named by any language. Languages may have verbal labels for between two and eleven colours.

Fuzzy boundary: members may be identified as belonging to different concepts, depending on the context in which we think about them.

General problem solver: Newall, Shaw and Simon's early computer model of thinking and means-end analysis.

Goal-directed thinking: the manipulation of symbols in order to solve a problem.

Graphemic knowledge: knowledge about the correspondence between written letters and their sounds.

Iconic representation: the second stage in Bruner's theory of thinking, in which children think in images.

Imaginative thinking: McKellar's term for rational and logical thinking which involves the manipulation of symbols.

Inference: this helps us to understand the language we hear. We draw on our general knowledge and previous experience of the world in order to add meaning to utterances. For example, if someone says they are going for a picnic you make inferences about the weather, about the food they might eat and so on.

Inner speech: term used by Vygotsky to describe the way in which children's speech about actions and plans gradually becomes internalized.

Internalized grammar: a term used by linguists to describe sound, word and meaning patterns which we all need in order to produce and understand language.

Language: Brown (1973) defines language as a communication system which must have semanticity, the capacity for displacement and productivity.

Lateral thinking: looking at a problem from many different angles.

Lexical knowledge: knowing what individual words mean.

Linguistic determinism: the strong form of the Sapir-Whorf hypothesis which states that language determines thought.

Linguistic relativity: the weaker form of the Sapir-Whorf hypothesis which states that language influences thinking.

Logical thinking: used in mathematics, philosophy and to construct reasoned arguments.

Means-end analysis: a process used to solve problems in which a problem is broken down into a series of steps (means) which lead to a solution (end).

Morphological knowledge: knowledge about how individual sounds within a language are combined into larger units called morphemes.

Particularistic meanings: Bernstein uses this phrase to describe the way in which restricted code speakers tend to rely on their listener's existing knowledge of the situation to which they are referring.

Phonological knowledge: knowledge of how the sounds of a language can be combined to form words.

Pragmatics: the functions of language, that is, what we use language for.

Pre-intellectual language: the term used by Vygotsky to describe children's early language development at the babbling stage, before language and thinking merge and develop together.

Pre-linguistic thought: children's earliest thinking which consists of actions, perceptions and images, according to Vygotsky.

Probabilistic concept: concepts in which members do not always share the same properties.

Productivity: in order to be a language, a communication system must have the capacity to combine a limited number of sounds or signs into an effectively unlimited number of messages.

Proposition: verbal information in the form of a statement, for example, 'Birds have wings'.

Prototype: an abstract representation of a concept member against which we match further examples as we experience them.

Restricted code: Bernstein's term referring to the type of language which tends to be used by working-class children to convey particularistic meanings.

Schemas: packets of information representing our general knowledge about objects, situations, events or actions.

Script: Schank uses this term to describe the way in which everyday routines are represented in memory as the result of past experiences. Scripts contain stored information about what is likely to happen in familiar situations.

Script Applier Mechanism: a computer program devised by Schank and his colleagues to demonstrate how scripts help us to understand familiar situations.

Semanticity: objects, events, emotional states and abstractions can be represented symbolically, that is, by words, so that the words mean the same things to all speakers of a language.

Semantic networks: meanings are thought to be represented in our schemas as networks of interconnecting sets of ideas, rather like an encyclopaedia.

Social context: language often requires information about the situation in which it is being used if its meaning is to be clear.

Social speech: the term used by Vygotsky to describe children's development of speech for communicating with others as opposed to speech for expressing their own intentions and plans for action.

Speech acts: Searle's term describing functions fulfilled by language.

Symbolic representation: the third stage in Bruner's theory during which children begin to think symbolically, a skill which requires mastering language.

Syntax: the grammar of a language which enables us to produce utterances which will be understood by other people.

Thinking: the mental processes involved in reasoning, problem solving, and the atttempt to make sense out of circumstances or events which happen to us, or which we hear about from others.

Transformational grammar: Chomsky's theory in which he attempts to describe the rules which he believes humans must 'know' in order to produce an infinite number of sentences.

Universalistic meanings: the term used by Bernstein to describe the way in which users of elaborated code express relationships between events and ideas so that everyone understands them. He believed that language used in this way fosters higher levels of thinking.

ANSWERS TO SELF-ASSESSMENT QUESTIONS

SAQ 1 (a) The three features are semanticity, displacement and productivity.

(b) The chimpanzees displayed semanticity, some displacement and limited productivity in their communication when taught sign language but there is little evidence that other systems of animal communication fulfil any of Brown's criteria for language.

(c) When signing, chimpanzees do not always use grammatical constructions consistently.

SAQ 2 You would need phonological, lexical, syntactic and semantic knowledge plus general knowledge about picnics and the weather.

SAQ 3 (a) is a command
(b) is a request
(c) is a statement
(d) is an apology.

SAQ 4
lexical knowledge	— what words mean
syntax	— grammatical rules
phonemes	— sounds of a language
speech acts	— functions of a language
morphemes	— words or parts of words
semantics	— rules governing meanings.

SAQ 5 (a) *The boy hit the ball*

1. S → NP & VP   The sentence (S) can be rewritten as a noun phrase (NP) plus a verb phrase (VP). The NP is *'The boy'* and the VP is *'hit the ball'*.

2. NP → Art & N   The noun phrase can be rewritten as an article (*the*) and a noun (*boy*).

3. VP → V & NP   The verb phrase can be rewritten as a verb (*hit*) and a noun phrase (*the ball*).

4. NP → Art & N   This is the same rule as 2, but in this case the noun is *ball*.

(b) By the grammar of our language, Chomsky means the system of rules about combining words into sentences which mean something. We need to share this system with other speakers of our language if we are to understand what they say to us and if we are to produce utterances which they will understand.

SAQ 6 Our picnic schema helps us to understand what is being said because it contains the information that picnics are meals which are eaten outside. We associate picnics with sunny, summer days. If the sky is overcast, we know from past experience that it might rain which will hinder us.

SAQ 7 (a) Schank believes that we build up a store of information relating to familiar routine situations, such as visiting restaurants. We then draw on this information to guide our expectations about what will happen when we are in a similar situation. In turn, this helps to guide our behaviour, based on our previous experience in similar situations. He calls the accumulation of information a script.

(b) Schank believes that meaning and syntax are inextricably linked in our schemas.

SAQ 8 The concept chair is probabilistic since not all chairs share the same characteristics. For example, some chairs are hard, some are soft, some have arms, some do not.

SAQ 9 Labov's results:

Drawing 1: all people in the *neutral* and *coffee* conditions, and most of those in the *food* and *flower* conditions gave the reponse 'cup'.

Drawing 2: all *neutral* and most *coffee* people continued to give the response 'cup' but only 60% of the *food* group and 50% of the *flower* group were still calling the receptacle a cup.

Drawings 3 & 4: the percentage of 'cup' responses for the *food* and *flower* groups were very low. People now tended to call the container 'bowl' and 'vase'. Even people in the *neutral* and *coffee* conditions were no longer calling the object a cup very often.

N.B. The responses change gradually from one drawing to the next which suggests that the boundaries to the 'cup', 'vase' and 'bowl' concepts are fuzzy, not clear cut.

SAQ 10 (a) Information may be represented in memory as automatic physical skills (often referred to as 'motor schemas'), images, mental models or propositions.

(b) Concepts are necessary for thinking because they enable us to categorize our world in ways that simplify and organize the vast amounts of information we have to deal with. Abstract concepts, based on words, permit thinking about abstract ideas which would not otherwise be possible.

SAQ 11 (a) Piaget believed that intelligence develops from birth through modification of existing schemas and the creation of new ones. Initially, this occurs through our physical interactions with the environment which results in the realization that our physical movements influence that environment. As our schemas become more complex, so too does our thinking.

(b) By egocentric speech, Piaget meant that young children's language reflects their intentions, motives and feelings. It is not used to communicate with other people but as a means of articulating their own thought processes aloud.

SAQ 12 (a) The strong version of the Sapir-Whorf hypothesis would state that if you did not have verbal labels for all the colours, then you would be unable to distinguish any shades of colour other than those you had names for — that is to say, language *determines* the way we categorize the world.

(b) The weak version states that language only *influences* thought. In this case, you would be able to distinguish the colours but might not have names for all of them.

SAQ 13 Carroll and Casagrande's experiment supports the strong version of Sapir-Whorf because it demonstrates how Navaho Indian language, which stresses the form of objects, determines thinking. Children brought up in a culture with such a language should be able to think about the form of objects better than children brought up in a culture whose language does not stress this aspect of their environment. This is what Carroll and Casagrande found, that children who spoke only Navaho were better at recognizing the form of objects than American children who spoke only English or those who spoke both Navaho and English. However, this conclusion should be treated with caution as the English-only children did better than children who spoke both Navaho and English which is surprising since the latter group had also been exposed to the language stressing form. This finding casts doubt on the conclusion that language determines thought.